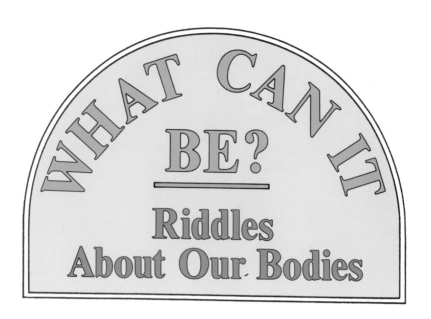

WHAT CAN IT BE?

Riddles About Our Bodies

Jacqueline A. Ball
&
Ann D. Hardy

Silver Press

Published by Silver Press, a division of Silver Burdett Press, Inc.
Simon & Schuster, Inc.
Prentice Hall Bldg., Englewood Cliffs, NJ 07632.
Printed in the United States of America.

10 9 8 7 6 5 4 3 2 1

Library of Congress Cataloging-in-Publication Data
Ball, Jacqueline A.,   Date.
    Ann Hardy
    Riddles about our Bodies
        p. cm. (What can it be?)
Summary: A collection of rhyming riddles about the parts of the human body.
1. Body, Human———Juvenile literature.   [1. Body, Human.
        2. Riddles.]   I. Hardy, Ann.
    II. Title.   III. Title: Riddles about our bodies.
    IV. Series: Ball, Jacqueline A., What can it be?
        QM27.B35 1989   611

ISBN 0–671–68579–1   89–6188
ISBN 0–671–68578–3 (lib. bdg.)   CIP   AC

WHAT CAN IT BE? concept created by Jacqueline A. Ball
PHOTO CREDITS:
    Cover (clockwise from upper left): Bruce Coleman, Inc./Jonathan T. Wright; COMSTOCK/Comstock; COMSTOCK/Michael Stuckey; Bruce Coleman, Inc./David Madison.
    Interior (in order of appearance): Bruce Coleman, Inc./Jonathan T. Wright, *insert of tongue* © Margaret Cubberly/PHOTOTAKE; Bruce Coleman, Inc./David Falconer; Bruce Coleman, Inc./D. P. Hershkowitz; COMSTOCK/Comstock; COMSTOCK/Michael Stuckey, *insert of lung* © Peter A. Simon/PHOTOTAKE; Bruce Coleman, Inc./Harry Hartman; Bruce Coleman, Inc./David Madison; COMSTOCK/Comstock, *insert of heart* © Peter A. Simon/ PHOTOTAKE; Bruce Coleman, Inc./Andrew Dalsimer; Bruce Coleman, Inc./Willy Spiller, *insert of stomach* © Peter A. Simon/ PHOTOTAKE; Bruce Coleman, Inc./Norman Owen Tomalin, *insert of brain* © CNRI/PHOTOTAKE; Bruce Coleman, Inc./Steve Solum; COMSTOCK/Chuck Mason; Bruce Coleman, Inc./Pat Lanza Field; Bruce Coleman, Inc./Pat Lanza Field.

BOOK DESIGN
Cover: Helen Tullen, Nancy S. Norton / *Interior:* Nancy S. Norton

I'm tucked in a cave,
Where I rest on the floor
'Til it's time to eat,
And you open the door.
Then my bumps take charge,
Helping you taste
Popcorn and pickles,
And minty toothpaste.

What am I?

YOUR TONGUE

Your tongue is covered with tiny taste buds. They tell your brain whether your food is sweet, sour, salty, or bitter.

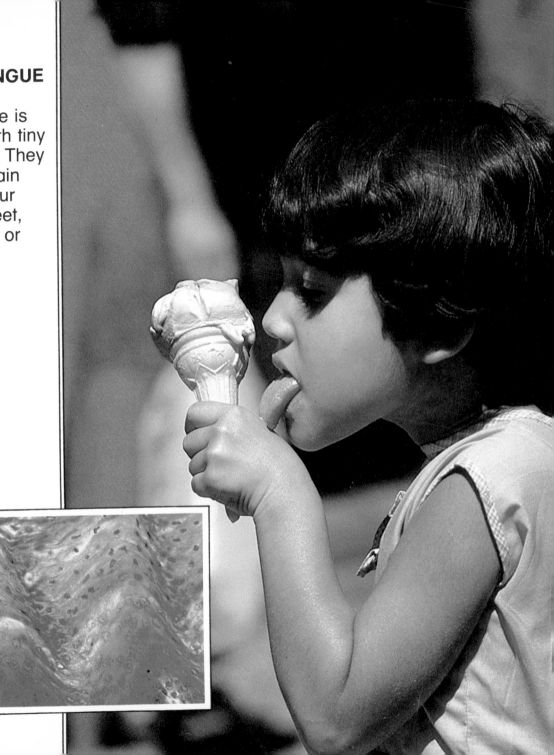

Raindrops racing on windowpanes,
Daffodils dancing on country lanes,
White smoke streaming from fast freight trains.
These are just three
     Of the pictures you see
          When you use me!

What am I?

YOUR EYES

Most people blink their eyes 25 times per minute. Blinking helps keep the eyes clean and protects them from anything that comes too close.

Spreads and blankets,
Quilts of down,
Cover you gently
From ankles to crown.

I cover you, too,
With a fit tight as glue!
But I stretch
While you smile
Or you frown.

What am I?

YOUR SKIN

Skin is made up of two main layers. The outer layer contains the pigment that gives your skin its color. The inner layer contains the nerves that help you to feel hot and cold.

What holds a pencil,
Scratches a head,
Tickles a tummy,
Picks up gingerbread?

They have swirls and squiggles,
And help you to feel
A soft bunny's tail,
Or a slippery eel.

What are they?

YOUR FINGERS

Your fingertips have thousands of nerve endings that help you to feel. The skin on your fingertips makes a pattern called a fingerprint. No two sets of fingerprints are the same.

Leapfrog, hopscotch
Puff . . . puff
Baseball, soccer
Huff . . . huff

What works much harder
When you're at play?
They help blow out candles
On your birthday!

YOUR LUNGS

Your lungs breathe in clean air which your blood then carries to every part of your body.

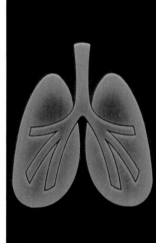

What can it be, do you suppose,
That's north of your knees
And far from your toes?
You need it to sneeze
Or to sniff a rose.
And when a skunk is nearby,
It knows!

YOUR NOSE

Your nose is
lined with a
membrane that
contains tiny
hairs. The hairs
filter out germs
from the air you
breathe. A
sneeze blows
out dust and dirt!

When I am straight,
I'm just at rest.
It's when I'm bent
That I work best.
I let you skip and skate and ski
And kick a ball! I am your ____.

KNEE

Your knee is the largest joint in your body. It is protected by your kneecap, which is shaped like a triangle.

Four small rooms
With pounding walls
Push red streams
Down long dark halls.
The size of your fist,
A powerful muscle,
It beats much faster
When you hustle and bustle.

What is it?

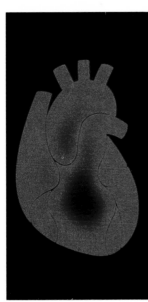

YOUR HEART

Your heart
weighs less than
a pound and
usually beats
about 70 times
per minute.
Exercise
keeps the
heart healthy!

You might think I'm scary
On Halloween,
But I'm very useful
All the times in between.
I'm the shape that supports you
Under your skin.
The name of this frame?
It's your _____ .

SKELETON
(Bones)

The largest bone
in your body is
your thigh bone.
The smallest is
in your ear and
is no bigger than
a grain of rice.

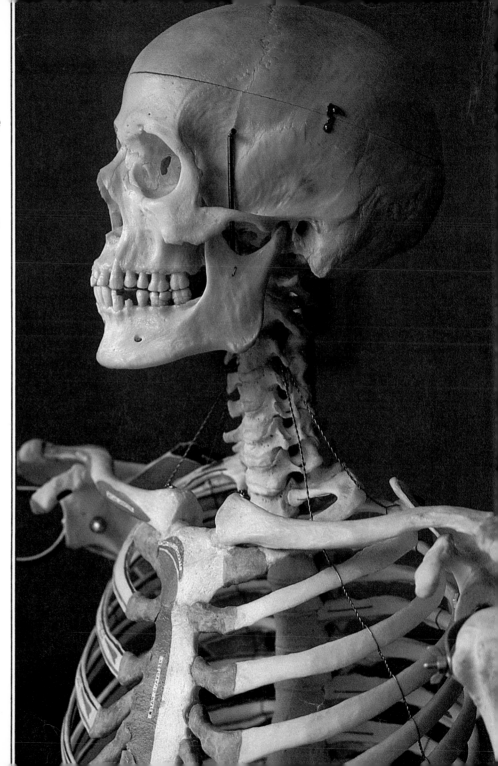

Cookies, yum!
Down they come.
Down they drop,
Riding,
Colliding,
Tumbling and sliding
'Til the grumbling inside
Finally stops!

Where are the cookies going?

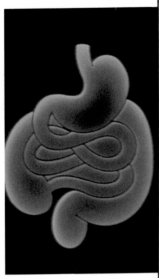

TO YOUR STOMACH

Your stomach helps change the food you eat to energy that you can use. It mixes the food with stomach fluids so it can move along.

I'm like a computer
In your head.
I'm why you remember
The words someone said.
I help you to separate
Blue things from red.
To think is my task,
Answer questions you ask,
And make dreams
While you're sleeping in bed.

What am I?

YOUR BRAIN

Your brain is the control center of your body. It stores information about everything that happens to you.

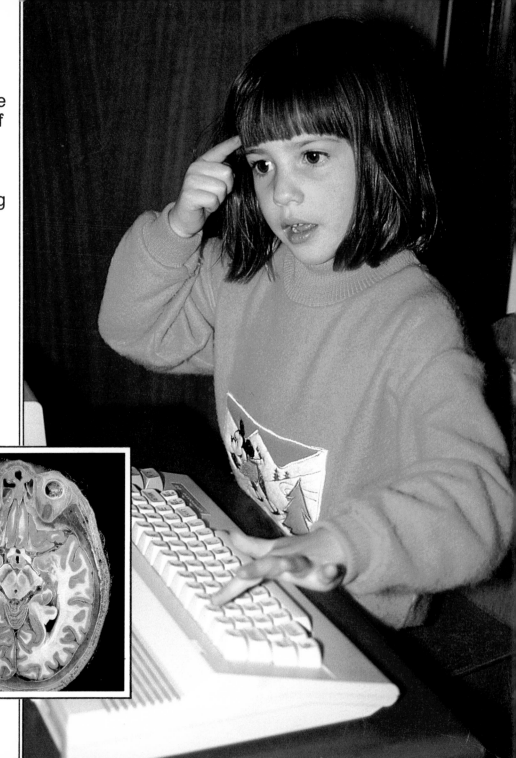

The pipe organ music
Of a carousel,
The buzzing of bees,
The chime of a bell,
The wind ruffling willows
When a big storm is near—
All of these sounds
I make perfectly clear.
I am your ____.

EAR

Sound travels into your ear on invisible waves. The waves make your eardrum vibrate. The vibrations travel to your brain, where they are changed into sounds you can understand.

Fine straight threads
Or a sea of waves.
It takes some teeth
To make them behave.

Long or short,
Thick or thin.
Can you count all the colors
That they come in?

What are they?

HAIRS

Hair can be straight, wavy, or curly. It depends on the angle from which the hair grows out of your scalp. It also depends on the shape of the hair's *follicle,* which is the place that surrounds the hair's root.

When I'm on top,
I like to chop.
When I'm behind,
I'd rather grind.

Not black, but white.
Not bark, but bite.
It's the honest truth,
I am your ____.

TOOTH

When you grow
up you'll have 32
permanent teeth.
A tooth is made
up of a crown,
which is the part
you see, and
roots that go
deep into the
gums.

For each move you make—
Every shiver and shake,
Every cough, every sneeze—
You need these.

So lift some weights to make them strong.
With exercise, you can't go wrong!

What are they?

YOUR MUSCLES

Your body has more than 600 muscles. Some are fastened to your bones and help you move. Others help you breathe and smile.